LEVEL 3

Written by: Rachel Wilson
Series Editor: Melanie Williams

T0386025

Pearson Education Limited
Edinburgh Gate, Harlow,
Essex CM20 2JE, England
and Associated Companies throughout the world.

ISBN: 978-1-4479-4435-5

This edition first published by Pearson Education Ltd 2013
5 7 9 10 8 6
Text copyright © Pearson Education Ltd 2013

The moral rights of the author have been asserted
in accordance with the Copyright Designs and Patents Act 1988

Set in 17/21pt OT Fiendstar
Printed in China
SWTC/05

Acknowledgements
The publisher would like to thank the following for their kind permission to reproduce their photographs:
(Key: b-bottom; c-center; l-left; r-right; t-top)

Alamy Images: Ryan M. Bolton 14t, Picture Hooked / Malcolm Schuyl 10r, Picture Press 7, 24/d (caterpillar);
Ardea: Francois Gohier 15tr, 24/b (egg); **Corbis:** DLILLC 13, Tim Fitzharris / Minden Pictures 21, 24/c (frog),
SA Team / Foto Natura / Minden Pictures 12; **FLPA Images of Nature:** Murray Cooper / Minden Pictures 20,
24/a (froglet), Chris Newton 9tl, 9tr, 9cl, 9cr, Malcolm Schuyl 10l, Christian Ziegler / Minden Pictures 16tl, 16b;
Fotolia.com: fovito 5t, hirron 11, M. Schuppich 4-5bl, 24/b (butterfly); **Getty Images:** Michael & Patricia Fogden
17, 24/d (tadpole), Adam Jones 14b, Rick Lew 22, Travelpix Ltd 15b, Martin Woike / Foto Natura 8;
Nature Picture Library: Simon Colmer 9br, 24/a (chrysalis); **SuperStock:** Loop Images 3,
Minden Pictures 6, 18-19, 24/c (egg)

Cover images: Front: **Fotolia.com**: M. Schuppich t; **Shutterstock.com**: Eric Isselée bl

All other images © Pearson Education

In some instances we have been unable to trace the owners of copyright material,
and we would appreciate any information that would enable us to do so.

Illustrations: Bernice Lum (The Organisation)

Published by Pearson Education Ltd

For a complete list of the titles available in the Pearson English Kids Readers series, please go to
www.pearsonenglishkidsreaders.com. Alternatively, write to your local Pearson Education office or to
Pearson English Readers Marketing Department, Pearson Education, Edinburgh Gate, Harlow, Essex CM202JE, England.

Hello and welcome. My name is Hannah, and I'm a scientist. I study animals. I want to show you two animals with amazing life cycles. The first is a butterfly, and it lives across Europe. Let's take a look.

life cycle the different stages of an animal's life

This is the Peacock butterfly. The pattern on its wings is beautiful, but it's also important. The circles look like eyes. Bigger animals than the butterfly are scared of the "eyes." To a mouse, it can look like a bird's head!

wing

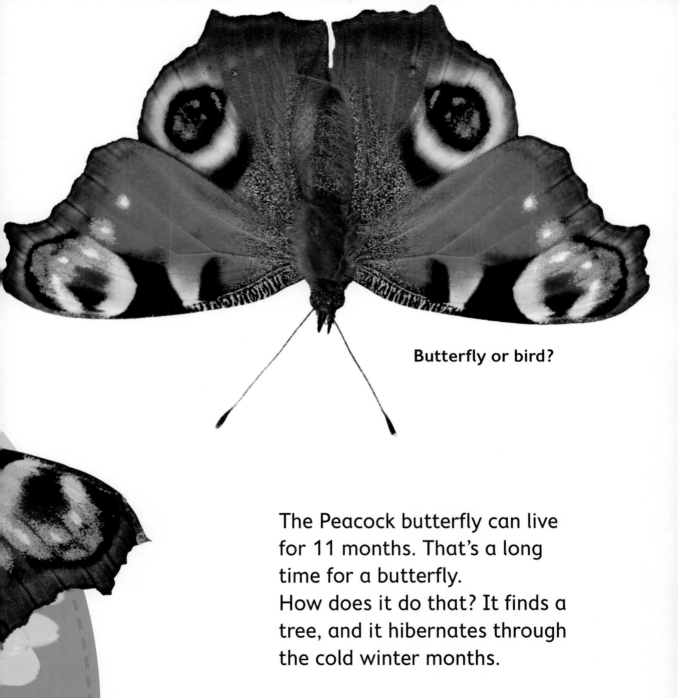

Butterfly or bird?

The Peacock butterfly can live for 11 months. That's a long time for a butterfly.
How does it do that? It finds a tree, and it hibernates through the cold winter months.

hibernate sleep through the winter

In the spring, the Peacock butterfly emerges from hibernation.
This is the first stage of its life cycle. First, the butterfly finds a mate. Then, it finds a plant in a sunny place and lays its eggs on the leaves.
The eggs are green and very small.

After about ten days, black caterpillars come out of the eggs. This is the second stage of the life cycle. The caterpillars are hungry, and they eat the leaves around them.

caterpillar

The caterpillars grow bigger and bigger every day. Now, they have to be careful. This is a dangerous time because birds can easily see them — and eat them!

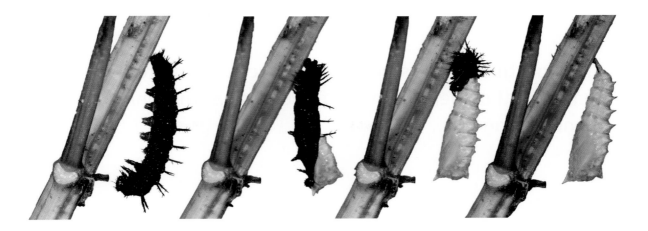

The third stage in the life cycle is amazing because the caterpillar changes. It grows a chrysalis around its body.

Why don't animals eat the chrysalis? They *want* to eat it ..., but they can't *see* it! The chrysalis looks like a leaf. That's smart!

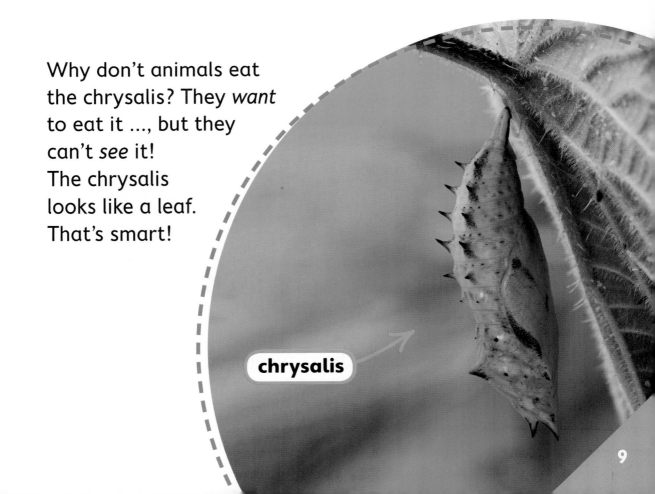

chrysalis

The fourth and last stage of the life cycle is more amazing than before. Inside the chrysalis, this animal is changing again ...

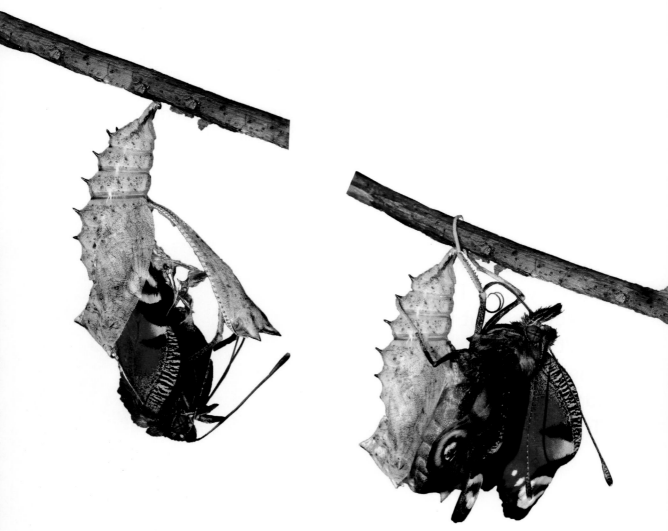

After about two weeks, the chrysalis slowly opens.
A new Peacock butterfly emerges. At first, it has to wait.
It can't fly because its wings are wet.

It's summer now. The butterfly flies from flower to flower. It has to eat a lot before the fall, and it's time to hibernate.

The Red-eyed tree frog is nocturnal. It lives in the trees, and it's good at jumping and climbing. Its feet can stick to the leaves.

It has some amazing colors on its body ...
    big red eyes,
    orange or red feet,
    a bright green body, and
    a blue and yellow pattern on its body.
That's a lot of colors for a small frog!

nocturnal awake at night

The colors on the Red-eyed tree frog are beautiful and also *important*. In the day, it sleeps on a green leaf. Animals can't see it because it looks like the leaf. Its big red eyes can scare bigger animals.

In the rainy season, the frog finds a mate. Then, it finds a leaf above a pond and lays its eggs.
The eggs stick to the leaf. This is the first stage of the frog's life cycle.

pond

rainy season in the rainy season, it rains every day

insect

snake

This is a dangerous time in the Red-eyed tree frog's life cycle. Snakes and big insects want to eat the eggs.

After some days, all the eggs open, and tadpoles emerge. This is the second stage in the frog's life cycle. The tadpoles slide down the leaf and drop into the water below.

tadpole

The tadpoles live in the water, and they eat very small insects. They have tails, and they look more like fish than frogs!

The third stage in the life cycle is amazing because the tadpole changes its body.

froglet

back legs

front legs

The tadpole is growing and changing. First, it grows back legs. Then, it grows front legs. It has a tail, but this is also changing. The tail is getting smaller and smaller.

Slowly the tadpole changes to a small brown froglet.
A froglet is a very young frog. It doesn't breathe under
water now. It comes out of the water and breathes.

The froglet moves from the water to the plants around the water. Its front and back legs get stronger, and it can climb now.

Slowly this small froglet changes from brown to the bright colors of the adult frog. This is the fourth and last stage of the frog's life cycle.

The sky is dark. The Red-eyed tree frog wakes up. It's time to catch an insect for breakfast.

What did you think? These are two amazing stories of animal life cycles. There are four stages for the butterfly and four stages for the frog, but they are very different. Can you remember them?

Before You Read

1 Look at the cover.
What can you see?

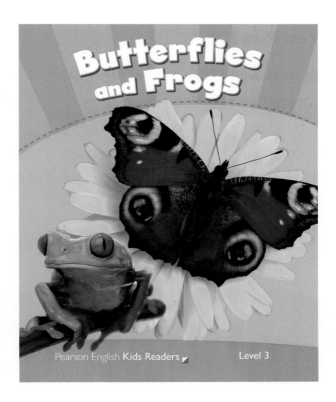

2 Look at these words. Find a picture of them in the book.

a caterpillar
b chrysalis
c tadpole
d insect
e froglet

Activity page ❷

After You Read

1 **Read and write Yes (Y) or No (N).**
   a Butterflies and frogs lay eggs.
   b A tadpole grows a tail and legs.
   c A caterpillar emerges from a chrysalis.
   d A froglet can breathe under the water.
   e A froglet is a young frog.

2 **Put the frog's life cycle in the right order.**
   ⓐ froglet   ⓑ egg   ⓒ frog   ⓓ tadpole

   Stage 1 =   Stage 2 =   Stage 3 =   Stage 4 =

3 **Put the butterfly's life cycle in the right order.**
   ⓐ chrysalis   ⓑ butterfly   ⓒ egg   ⓓ caterpillar

   Stage 1 =   Stage 2 =   Stage 3 =   Stage 4 =